ACTIVATE YOUR FAITH

*God has purposed you for great and
amazing things*

Dr. Robert L. Lawson

Gotham Books

30 N Gould St.
Ste. 20820, Sheridan, WY 82801
https://gothambooksinc.com/

Phone: 1 (307) 464-7800

© 2023 *Dr. Robert L. Lawson.* All rights reserved.

No part of this book may be reproduced, stored in a retrieval system, or transmitted by any means without the written permission of the author.

Published by Gotham Books (June 20, 2023)

ISBN: 979-8-88775-337-9 (H)
ISBN: 979-8-88775-335-5 (P)
ISBN: 979-8-88775-336-2 (E)

Because of the dynamic nature of the Internet, any web addresses or links contained in this book may have changed since publication and may no longer be valid.

The views expressed in this work are solely those of the author and do not necessarily reflect the views of the publisher, and the publisher hereby disclaims any responsibility for them.

Table Of Contents

Introduction 1

Activate Your Faith 6

Spiritual Sagacity... 7

Spiritual Insights and Wisdom.. 9

The Walk of Faith... 12

Against All Odds 15

Integrity 16

The Thought and Faith Factors in Achievement............... 17

Keep Digging.. 20

Thoughts.. 22

The Chosen Vessel 24

An Analysis of the Chosen Vessel.................................... 26

The Ingredients of Faith 29

Preparation Is the Key to Success..................................... 31

Spiritual Wisdom.. 37

Momentum 38

Power.. 39

The Phenomenal Encourager 44

Endurance... 48

Moving Forward in Faith.. 55

Leadership, Faith and Transformation.............................. 59

The Power of Transformation... 63

God's Plan and Purpose... 65

God Knows Best.. 66

Faith... 69

The Case for Christ.. 70

God's Grace... 76

God Has Purposed You for Great and Amazing Things...... 77

Closing Thoughts.. 78

About the Author 80

Introduction

"And Jabez called on the God of Israel, saying, Oh that thou wouldest bless me indeed, and enlarge my coast, and that thine hand might be with me, and that thou wouldest keep me from evil, that it may not grieve me. And God granted him that which he requested." Ist Chronicles 4:10. Wow! How powerful is that?

Normally, when I write a book, I generally write the introduction first. However, that was not the case with this book. I was several chapters into the heart of this book before God began speaking to me about what should go into the introduction.

As I listened intently to his voice, he began dropping jewels of wisdom into my mind that consisted of verses, quotes, poems and thoughts that might prove to be of significant value to others as they read the content and what his desire is to pour out to you, the reader, while all the time using me as a vessel to get his point across to you.

Perhaps God wants you to know that everyone travels a different path in life. Many experiences are relatable to what others are going through and many are not. Perhaps God wants you to know that he is the same God that exists today as he was in the day of the prophet Jabez. What if you entered his presence and prayed the same prayer that Jabez prayed? Are you ready for what could happen? God never changes. He is the one constant you can depend on and he works through you to reach others as he continually manifests his word in your heart. Great blessings can be bestowed upon others as a result of that. That has always been his intent. The more obedient we become to the promptings of the Holy Spirit, the more God can use every single one of us to convict others through the power of his holy presence.

I kept thinking about the types of individuals who might pick up this book and read it. I thought about ministers who've been preaching the word of God their entire lives and of how critical they might be of what they find written here. I thought about

Christians and about non-Christians who might not know the first thing about God. Suddenly, God shifted my paradigm and limited way of thinking and changed my entire thought process. That's when his wisdom began to flow through me. It became clear and evident to me that this book project was far bigger and far more encompassing than my own limited thinking or the limited thinking of others. God explained to me in no uncertain terms that only his thoughts were the ones that mattered. He placed the words of Theodore Roosevelt on my heart.

"It is not the critic who counts. It is not the man who points out where the strong man stumbled or whether the doer of great deeds could have done them better. The credit belongs to the individual who is actually in the arena, whose face is marred with dust and sweat and blood, who strives valiantly, who errs, who comes up short again and again and again but who while daring greatly spends himself in a worthy cause so that his place may not be among those cold and timid souls who know neither victory nor defeat."

In other words, my friends, stop listening to the critics and start listening to him. Start believing in him, start believing in yourself and start doing all of those things you never thought you could do. This is the most powerful way in which you can break through every barrier of limitation and resistance that seeks to inhibit any aspect of your own personal and professional growth and development. God is the answer and not man. Listen to his voice that will direct and guide you. If it is good, it is of God.

The Bible tells us in 1st Corinthians 14:33, "For God is not the author of confusion, but of peace, as in all churches of the saints." Stop thinking of the church building as the sanctuary. If you have been saved, the Holy Spirit resides in you. You are the church in which the Holy Spirit manifests itself. The building in which you attend church is merely the physical edifice where people gather to worship and praise God. The body of Christ (you) is what goes out into the various places in the community to spread the word of God every day through your disposition in your encounters with others and through the ways in which you act.

God is not the author of division, strife, enmity and confusion. God is about unity and demonstrating to others how they can work together effectively. That latter part is when you know that something is of God.

When you do something positive, good and uplifting that helps others to grow, you may be looked upon favorably by your brothers and sisters and people may say that you are doing a good job and they may motivate and inspire you by their kind words and support but that should not be why you do what you do. In the end, all that is going to matter is this one thing. It is evident in Colossians 3:23. "And whatsoever ye do, do it heartily, as to the Lord and not unto men."

When you examine or look at your works and what you are doing, all you have to do is think about it in relationship to God's intent and not man's. This is what enables and empowers you to transcend their criticism. God is far above all of them. In the end, you want to savor the flavor and squeeze out all the juice that God has placed in you. Get it out. Stop worrying about what others think and begin thinking about what God's plan might be for your life.

When you make the transition from this life into eternity, you can rest assured that your mind is not going to be focused on the critics and what others are thinking of you. You'll be thinking about yourself, your family and all of those who've loved you over the years and perhaps a little about the legacy you might be leaving that others can build on.

Perhaps one of your questions to self might be. Did I do everything I could within my power to reach and share with as many people as I could? Am I satisfied with my contribution? Could I have done more? If so, what? Let me leave you with these wise words of Dale Wimbrow.

The Man in the Glass

When you get what you want in your struggle for self,
And the world makes you King for a day;
Just go to a mirror and look at yourself,
And see what that man has to say.

For it isn't your brother, or mother or wife,
Whose judgment upon you must pass;
But the one whose verdict counts most in your life,
Is the one staring back from the glass.

Some people may think you're a straight shootin chum,
And call you a wonderful guy;
But the man in the glass says you're only a bum,
If you can't look him straight in the eye.

He's the fellow to please, never mind all the rest,
For he's with you clear up to the end,
And you've passed your most dangerous, difficult test,
If the man in the glass is your friend.

You may fool the whole world on the pathway of life,
And get pats on your back as you pass;
But your final reward will be heartaches and tears,
If you've cheated the man in the glass.

This book is all about the activation of your faith. It's all about your ability to increase your belief level in yourself and in what God has designed you to do. Faith is belief through demonstrated action and the time for action is now. You can win souls to Christ by showing how God has been a factor in your life and how his influence over your thoughts and actions has played a significant role in the person you've become and in the quality of the life you live. This is the kind of experience you can share that will have a powerful impact on others with whom you have the opportunity to interact. Your ability to enhance and improve the quality of life for others through your testimony for God and how he has worked in your life is what ultimately creates a manifest hope in the hearts of others.

It becomes as the great poet Emily Dickinson has said, "Hope is the thing with feathers that perches in the soul. It sings the tune without the words and never stops at all." Anyone who encounters God becomes a purveyor of hope and soon realizes that God has purposed them for great and amazing things.

Activate Your Faith

Perhaps the only reason,
You have yet to make your mark;
Lies solely with the fact that,
You keep shooting in the dark.

You say that you believe,
In your talent and your skill;
And there is much you can achieve,
When you apply your human will.

God showers you with mercy,
And the fullness of his grace;
But miracles unfold,
When you activate your faith.

The gifts that you inherit,
When you truly do believe;
Transcend the scope of reason,
Far beyond what you receive.

For the God who owns the cattle,
On a thousand distant hills;
Has the wherewithal to orchestrate,
Exactly what he wills.

His son whose broken body,
Hung on the cross to bleed;
Looked far beyond your faults,
To see exactly what you need.

Nothing is more powerful,
That his amazing grace;
And your mountains will be moved,
When you activate your faith.

Spiritual Sagacity

The knowledge and insights that I am about to share are taken directly from a segment of writing entitled "Forerunner Commentary." The passage was written and explained thoroughly by John W. Ritenbaugh.

In order for us to fully understand the powerful term, "sagacity," I believe it is essential and necessary to define the term. The term "sagacity" which entered the English language from Latin through French suggests "quickness of perception," soundness in judgment', and in farsightedness.

It pictures a mind that can cut through a situation's unimportant fluff or misdirecting false flags to grasp the essentials of a problem's solution. This is important for a Christian because the world is full of clever deceptions.

A Christian must understand that the wise solution in life is always to submit humbly to God in faith. We are to do this despite the twisted reasoning that can infiltrate our minds from a multitude of experiences in the worldly system.

The wise King Solomon gives us real-life examples of circumstances that arise in the world to present us with difficult choices. Because of our carnal nature, the foolish choice may often appear more attractive on the surface. Solomon shows us in bold strokes what Godly wisdom is and is not. He always makes clear what is and is not wise and he does that most clearly in those chapters in which he makes direct comparisons. "This is better than that." However, what may not appear at first glance is why this choice is better than that one. Godly wisdom does not always initially appear to be the wiser choice despite common human opinion.

A major lesson from the book of Ecclesiastes is that the wisdom Solomon is promoting is indeed sagacity. We have a tendency to think of wisdom as a quality possessed by those of higher educational levels, that is, it belongs to people who have achieved multiple university degrees, written some books, and sport a string of distinguishing letters after their name.

That distinction may suggest itself, but King Solomon has something else in mind. Though such people may have rightly earned respect from their peers, Solomon is concerned about day to day living regardless of who one is or what his station in life is. This implies that a measure of biblical wisdom is achievable by anybody whom God calls. Why? The source of this wisdom is God, who gives it as a gift to those who have a relationship with him. Here we find the most useful application of the wisdom of Ecclesiastes. Though helpful to anyone, it is primarily intended for those already in a relationship with God. "Whatsoever thy hand findeth to do, do it with thy might; for there is no work, nor device, nor knowledge, nor wisdom, in the grave, whither thou goest." Ecclesiastes 9:10.

Spiritual Insights and Wisdom

God resides in the spiritual realm for God is spirit. The spiritual dimension is the channel on which God sits......waiting for you to lend an ear to what he has to say. In the divine order of things, God can work with and through you when you allow yourself to be aligned with his holy will for your life. Your obedience to his promptings is a prime prerequisite for what he can and will do in your life. This is something that when you are in alignment with his perfect will for your life, surpasses all levels of human understanding.

Those who have no relationship with God cannot understand or discern these matters because they are spiritually dead. To them, the spiritual essence of life appears to be foolishness and wishful thinking. Little do they know how real the power of God is.

The relationship you develop with God is essential to the activation of your faith from a biblical perspective for he who cometh to God must believe that he is and that he is a rewarder of those who diligently seek him in order to ascertain his specific purpose for their lives.

God has a powerful desire for you to get beyond the words and specifically apply those words to your life. Knowing his specific will for your life requires that your level of trust in what he has to say and do is complete.

You must turn everything over to him and let him work his will in your life. Don't go into his presence praying for him to work a miracle and then open your eyes and continue holding onto the burdens you so clearly laid at his feet. If you've asked God to perform a miracle in your life, you must rest in his arms and relinquish your power, your authority and your control over the matter and simply trust that he will resolve the issue. In other words, do not pick your burdens back up, leave them in the hands of the master who has the ultimate power to resolve them. Let go and let God. If you are willing to walk in his will, God will guide your every step into truth and righteousness for his sake. You have to demonstrate the tenets of your faith through your actions.

God's spiritual nature has a supreme understanding of man's limited carnal nature because he operates in both the infinite and the finite world. He knew each of us prior to our being formed in the wombs of our mothers. His infinite wisdom is above all other forms of wisdom. His name is above all other names. God doesn't need any of us but is still willing to work with and through all of us in accordance with how strongly and intently we believe in who and what he actually is. The true essence of his dignity and nature is incomprehensible to anything known or unknown to man.

In the second part of 1st John 4:4 the scripture reads thus "Greater is he who is in you than he who is in the world." If you read the verse in its full context you will realize that John's intent is not that you can just go after your dreams without the assurance that God is behind you and pushing you to become a better version of yourself. There's an even deeper meaning at work here. This verse helps you to guard against false prophets, false teachers and charlatans who hide behind the word of God and use that same verse to spread false propaganda. When you try the true spirit of God that resides within you for itself, this is what knowing the true essence of God really means.

There is no substitute religion or agnostic belief that has the ability to usurp the power that resides in the God of Abraham, Isaac and Jacob. Rev. Antonio Neely, the current pastor of Pleasant Green Baptist Church would say it this way. "If you allow God to operate within you, he will show you your assignment." When you look closely at the conceptual framework and the ideological aspects of what constitutes your whole person – spirit- soul- body, that's when you can easily unravel the mystery of what it is that makes you whole.

The spirit aspect of your nature is your God consciousness. Spirit = God Consciousness. Secondly, when God created you, he made you from the dust of the earth and breathed life into your very being and you became a living soul. In other words, you literally became a living,

10

breathing human being. Soul = Self Consciousness. This second aspect of who you are is reflective of your human intellect. Your human intellect cannot outthink God which is precisely why everything stays in some sense of order. It is only when we think we know better than God that life becomes more difficult for us to manage effectively. When that happens, Proverbs 3:6 will enable us to get things back in proper order. "In all thy ways acknowledge him and he will direct thy paths."

The third aspect of our whole person represents the body or the physical attributes of who we are as God's creation. We are world conscious and engulfed in the material machine of this thing we call life. This includes our daily struggles, the societal norms that we challenge or that challenge us. It's the ebb and flow of life that we make decisions about on a daily basis.

The Walk of Faith

Prophecies are as old and as valid as the beginning of time itself. Now that I am older, it is much easier for me to reflect back over my life and see that when I thought I was in control, God was the one who was really ordering my steps and setting me up for success when I had no idea of what success really was. Realization has finally dawned on me that certain opportunities that had previously availed themselves to me were not my doing but God's. What a powerful and insightful revelation that has become.

In each instance, God had fully prepared me to embrace and take full advantage of each opportunity that presented itself. Since mom was not in a position to raise me when I was born, she did the next best thing. She gave me to my aunt and grandmother to raise and that one move in and of itself turned out to be a major blessing. My aunt made sure that I was fully aware of the Bible, all of its biblical applications and the teachings of Jesus Christ.

Certainly, like most of us, I've been up and down in my Christian walk but still, I was saved at the age of thirteen and accepted Jesus as my personal savior. To say that I strayed away from the teachings of Christ is an understatement. I struggle daily to keep the commandments but I won't permit that to keep me from growing closer to what his will and purpose is for my life on a daily basis. When I observe the world we live in today, I see it as an ongoing dilemma that affects us all. We struggle with our faith. We struggle with God and with temptation. Still, God has not withdrawn his hand of protection from me and has forever been the most influential voice in my life guiding my footsteps.

When the prophecies are shared with you early in life, they resonate as a distinctive and measurable truth. If they are powerful enough and you internalize them, the believability factor kicks in and it plays an incredible role in relationship to the power of expectancy.

When you buy into that prophecy, it becomes your standard of belief and your ability to prove its efficacy becomes paramount to your success. Efficacy is being defined here as "the ability to produce an intended result." If it is a powerful, productive and personal prophecy, that means that you will do everything within your power to bring that prophecy to fruition.

The most powerful prophecy that had the most significant impact upon my life occurred when I was very young. I don't remember exactly what age I was but my aunt, Nora Faye Lawson had a dream and, in that dream, an evangelist by the name of Ethel R. Willis appeared to her and shared with her four key words that would forever shape and mold me into the person God would have me to become over the years. Those words were, "Your boy cannot fail." Personally, I think how that statement is perceived and interpreted makes all the difference in the world. I never once interpreted it to mean that I couldn't fail a test, experience a major setback, get physically whipped or make numerous mistakes. I interpreted it to mean that no matter what I was confronted with that I would eventually emerge victorious when the end result was calculated.

To that end, throughout my grade school, high school and collegiate career, although I may have come close to failing on several occasions, that prophecy turned out to be perfectly true. I never failed a single grade and when I strove to obtain a baccalaureate, masters and doctoral degree, even when obstacles appeared to be insurmountable, God was always present to ensure my success at every level. Yes, of course, I had to do the work but God always made sure that I had the stamina, the ability and the persistence to follow through no matter what impediments I encountered along the way. Life can be cruel and harsh at times. If you've not experienced that yet, just keep living. There were instances and times where matters seemed impossible and insurmountable and yet, God, was always there to demonstrate his level of superior good will that enabled me to keep pressing on. It didn't hurt matters any when from time to time I could hear my aunt whispering the words of the prophet in my ear, "Your boy cannot fail."

Long before my wife, Deborah Lawson, placed the following words over the door of one of the rooms in our home, they were written in this book. What she did validated God's intent and purpose for my life and hers. His words can do the same for you. That's why I called this chapter, The Walk of Faith. So, what are those powerful, majestic and mystical words? "With God all things are possible."
Matthew 19:26

Against All Odds

When you've played the hand that you were dealt,
Against all odds it seems;
There may have come a time you felt,
To give up on your dreams.

But deep inside your beating heart,
The nature of your mind;
Would not allow that thought to grab,
A place to hold or find.

And so your will began to drive,
And mount a sturdy quest;
Resolved inside a thinking mind,
That you'd become your best.

Sometimes it takes that fire within,
To build on sturdy clods;
Inch by inch and yard by yard,
Fight hard against all odds.

There are stories by the thousands,
Of those who've overcome;
By staying in the race they start,
And daring still to run.

The magic of the moment,
Lies deep down in the pit;
It's when you're hit the hardest,
That you dare to find your grit.

When you've been battle tested,
And scarred by steel rods;
You can feel the satisfaction,
When you win against all odds.

Integrity

Your integrity is your moral compass. It operates as the center of your being. It is where the deepest truth resides. It is the one thing of value that connects all other values. When you are true to it, it will be true to you because of what you know you feel inside of yourself.

Integrity does not lie for it is truth. When you feel this deep conviction and it permeates your sensibilities, you must rest assured that nothing can stand in your way to prohibit you from achieving your objectives.

You will win it says because you already have. Other people just haven't seen it yet. It is your level of belief in this supreme quality of integrity that surpasses all other levels of human understanding.

It is incredulous. You know exactly what resides in your heart. It just becomes a matter of your having the discipline to stay the course until you have brought what you have been destined to do to fruition. Integrity is the superglue that makes you who you are. When others see it in operation, they will immediately recognize its authenticity. Nothing, absolutely nothing can withstand its power to draw. It's the piece that reflects your ability to win and no one can withstand its resolve.

The Thought and Faith Factors in Achievement

God has plans for you. "For I know the plans I have for you. Plans to prosper you and not to harm you. Plans to give you hope and a future. Jeremiah 29:11. Thought and faith are inextricably linked. If your mind dwells on the greatness of God and all that he has purposed you to do, there is absolutely nothing you cannot accomplish. Romans 8:28 will validate this for you even further. "All things work together for good to them that love the Lord and are the called according to his purpose. Your thought life is a reflection of who you are and who you are becoming. The more you are able to relinquish who you were yesterday, the more you can become the very person that God intended you to be in the first place.

The Reverend Bishop T.D. Jakes says it this way. "For I have not come clothed in the vesture of my past, nor will I use the opinions of this world for my defense. No, I am far wiser through the things I have suffered and I have come in my father's name. I am covered by his anointing, comforted by his presence and kept by his auspicious grace. Today as never before, I stand in the identity he has given me and I renounce every memory of who I was yesterday. I was called for such a time as this and I have come in my father's name."

You are constantly developing, constantly changing and constantly becoming a new creature in Christ Jesus each and every moment of your existence. Yesterday's thoughts and actions can eventually become obsolete to you. You do not have to remain a prisoner to your past behaviors and thoughts, not even those of just a few moments ago. The more you are able to break loose from the bonds of what holds you captive mentally, the freer your spirit becomes in order for you to activate your faith in becoming the highest representation of who Christ intended you to be.

The great Greek philosopher, Heraclitus, says it this way. "The soul is dyed the color of its thoughts. Think only on those things that are in line with your principles and can bear the full light of day. The content of your character is your choice. Day by day, what you choose, what you think and what you do is who you become. Your integrity is your destiny. It is the light that guides your way."

Achieving a life objective requires a full activation of faith. You must, as the astute and savvy businessman, Jim Rohn once said, "Stand guard at the door of your mind and control what goes in." You cannot allow yourself to be seduced by every distraction that comes your way. Those whims and fancies are impediments to your progress; they are barriers that prevent you from getting where you want to go. They disrupt your focus and forward thinking and cause you to delay what could be happening to you in life a lot sooner. This is precisely why the great writer, Ralph Waldo Emerson once said, "The ancestor of every action is a thought." The real key here is understanding what that thought is and why you are acting on it. Is it something that is getting you closer to your goal or is it something that is distracting you for a period of time? Only you can answer that question.

I'm not saying never take time to relax. Quite the contrary. Relaxation heals the soul, makes its essence wholesome and provides ample time for enjoyment and the recharging of your batteries. What I am saying is try to make sure you're not wasting an inordinate amount of time on trivial and mundane activities and pursuits. Let's face it though. Time is life and how you spend it is entirely up to you.

In Second Corinthians 10:5, it says, "Casting down imaginations, and every high thing that exalteth itself against the knowledge of God, and bringing into captivity every thought to the obedience of Christ." The very doing of this enables you to align your thinking in closer proximity to what God would have you to be.

Your prayer line is your direct connection to God and he stays on that line 24/7. He is never too busy to listen to what you have to say. It pleases him when you take a few moments to thank and praise him for what he has already done for you. The more grateful you are, the more it allows him to see your humility and your appreciation at work. Your attitude of gratitude is a reflection of one of the most powerful attributes of abundant living. A thankful heart is a righteous manifestation of God's sovereignty and power.

Conversing with God can be a very powerful and revealing thing. There are times when God wants us to be still so we can hear the soft tenderness of his voice as he takes the time to share and guide us in the direct way he wishes us to go. I am still here but it is only because of his abundant grace and mercy. Sometimes God is just there to provide you with the comfort and the support you need or are looking for especially when there is no one else you can depend on. God is amazing in the way that he demonstrates his love for us when we are perhaps at a low point in our lives.

I remember vividly once years ago when I was at a point in my life where I was feeling despondent and lost. I was having the pity party of my life. I didn't know which way to turn for some reason. I just felt like no one cared about what was happening in my life. I remember kneeling beside my bed. My Bible was on my bed and I just opened it to a page. It was at that precise moment that my eyes fell upon a specific verse, "Lo, I am with you always." Everything in my life changed at that moment. It was like having God breathe new life into me. I felt his presence in my room that night. What I experienced at that moment helped me to realize that God would never leave me nor forsake me no matter what. I remember getting up from the side of my bed. From that point forward everything was ok. God always has a way of reaching out to you and comforting you when you least expect it. What a mighty God we serve.

Keep Digging

A story once was told to me,
When you feel you've lost your grit;
Recharge your weakened batteries,
And never, never quit.

A house was filled with water,
And the owner lost his mind;
Because the source of all his problems,
Was the thing he could not find.

He called the water experts,
And they dug into the ground;
He had to pay so much a foot,
The cost was so profound.

Stop! He told the contractors,
I cannot stand the cost;
So they cut the rig, they stopped the dig,
And tried to stem the loss.

The owner was not happy,
Cause the problems still persist;
His thoughts were so confounded,
He said, "What the heck is this?"

So the owner soon relented,
And he told the man to dig,
So once again the experts,
Hooked up the sturdy rig.

This time they dug so deeply,
Over 1,000 feet;
The owner said, you've got to stop,
The price is just too steep.

When the digger got the message,
He had dug a little more;
Just four more lousy inches,
And they settled now the score.

A well deep in the earth,
On which the property set;
Was the culprit of the leakage,
That had hedged the owner's bet.

So when you're just about to quit,
And give up in despair;
Make sure you just keep digging,
Cause you're really almost there.

Thoughts

Let God guide you through the trials and tribulations. Let him manifest his plans, his ideas and his desires in your heart and then bring them to fruition. If you truly believe in God, he can and he will make all of it happen. It won't be on your time table that any of it occurs but on his. God will surely bring it to pass and he will do so in the proportion that he deems necessary and appropriate.

He first needs to discover whether or not you are a willing vessel that he can pour into and then out of. If you will take the time to relinquish your thoughts, get on his frequency and listen to his voice, you can then allow him to order your steps.
In psalms 46:10, he says, "Be still and know that I am God." He will easily and assuredly give you the plan that he has ultimately designed for your life. He provides yet more direction in Isaiah 40:31 when we become too anxious and impatient. "They that wait upon the Lord shall renew their strength. They shall mount up with wings as eagles. They shall walk and not be weary. They shall run and not faint."

Most people who read those words just gloss over them but if you take the time to just study them for a moment, such majestic and powerful revelations are hidden in those words. Just think for a moment the rejuvenation and energy that comes from waiting and not being in a hurry. Think of how your own individual power is being rekindled. That sense of renewed energy gives you the strength you need to overcome those obstacles that stand in your way. Just think of the power inherent in the wings of an eagle as it soars effortlessly through the sky. Just think of running and because you've taken the time to rest for a bit, that sense of renewed energy is what gives you the power to finish the race. That was God's initial intent for your life. "Being confident of this very thing, that he which hath begun a good work in you will perform it until the day of Jesus Christ. Philippians 1:6.

God has assembled a three-step process that helps to guide and facilitate what you are doing and where you are going. That

process begins with thought, it is activated and refined by your faith and is then implemented by the bonafide actions
that you take. God has to get your heart right with him first, which is why he had to confront Saul on the Damascus Road. He had to change Saul's heart in order to use him mightily. If he can do it for Saul, he can do it for you. The great prophet Mahatma Gandhi once said something very powerful. "It's the action, not the fruit of the action that's important. You have to do the right thing. It may not be in your power, may not be in your time, that there'll be any fruit. But that doesn't mean you stop doing the right thing. You may never know what results come from your action but if you do nothing, there will be no result."

It suffices to say that you do not control God. Rather, God controls you if you are obedient to his will for your life. Given that observation, that means that even when you cannot see the fruit, it doesn't mean you stop doing the right thing. You keep doing it anyway. When it's time for the proper manifestation to occur, it will. All of that remains within God's providence and his domain. He is literally the impetus behind what makes it all happen. Listen. Get ready for a real treat. This may be one of the best treats in the book. God enjoys using broken vessels to perform his works! His glory is uncanny and unbelievable. Broken vessels are God's greatest treasures. He uses them mightily to work through and perform his miracles. My own personal journey is incredibly dynamic, spiritual, deeply moving and powerful. If God can work in my life and do in my life what he has seen fit to do with me, what can he do with you?

The Chosen Vessel

Beulah V. Cornwell

The master was searching for a vessel to use.
On the shelf there were many, which one would he choose?
Take me cried the gold one, I'm shiny and bright
I'm of great value and I do things just right.
My beauty and luster will outshine the rest
And for someone like you master, gold would be best.

The master passed on with no word at all
He looked at a silver urn narrow and tall;
I'll serve you dear master, I'll pour out your wine
And I'll be at your table wherever you dine
My lines are so graceful, my carvings so true
And my silver will always compliment you.

Unheeded the master passed on to the brass,
It was wide mouthed and shallow and polished like glass
Here! Here! Cried the vessel, I know I will do
Place me on your table for all men to view.

Look at me called the goblet of crystal so clear,
My transparency shows my contents so dear,
Though fragile am I, I will serve you with pride,
And I'm sure I'll be happy in your house to abide.

The master came next to a vessel of wood
Polished and carved, it solidly stood.
You may use me dear master the wooden bowl said
But I'd rather you used me for fruit and not bread.

Then the master looked down and saw a vessel of clay,
Empty and broken it helplessly lay
No hope had the vessel that the master might choose
To cleanse and make whole, to fill and to use.

Ah! This is the vessel I've been hoping to find
I will mend it and use it and make it all mine
I need not the vessel with pride of itself;
Nor the one who is narrow to sit on the shelf
Nor the one who is big mouthed, shallow and loud
Nor one who displays his contents so proud:
Not the one who thinks he can do all things just right
But this plain earthly vessel filled with power and might.

Then gently he lifted the vessel of clay
Mended it and cleansed it and filled it that day
Spoke to it kindly. There's work you must do,
Just pour out to others as I pour into you.

An Analysis of the Chosen Vessel

The "Chosen Vessel" encourages and exemplifies exactly what God intends for each one of us to do. The more you have the ability to humble yourself in God's presence and demonstrate your thankfulness in showing your appreciation for how much he has already blessed you, the more he can utilize your talents, your gifts, your skills and your abilities in an exalted fashion to benefit others.

All you have to do is wait upon his lead for direction, guidance and purpose in your own life. If you have faith in him, if you believe in him and if you will activate your faith through prayer combined with effort in accordance with his specific will and purpose for your life, you can and will flourish at an unprecedented level of prosperity, honor and good will.

Jesus Christ will show you the way. He will show you exactly what he has planned for you to do. "But as it is written, eye has not seen, nor ear heard, neither have entered into the heart of man, the things which God hath prepared for them that love him. But God has revealed them to us by his spirit: for the spirit searcheth all things, yea, the deep things of God. 1st Corinthians chapter 2 verses nine and ten.

Unfortunately, so many people miss out on their true calling in life because they are simply too full of themselves to discover the real power inherent in God's word with which God has endowed but can only be revealed to them through his Holy Spirit. The "Chosen Vessel" speaks directly to so many people. Pride, arrogance and a lack of humility have been the downfall of so many.

Don't think for one moment that just because you've been downtrodden, perhaps thrown away, discarded as useless, rejected by many who refused to acknowledge you as a person because of your stature or lack of status in life that God thinks the way human beings do because he does not.

When God gets ready to shine the spotlight on you, he can easily elevate you to a level in society that most people can only dream about. God knows everything there is to know about you. He knows your every thought before you can even think it so his will for your life is far superior to the limited mindsets of those men and women who may be evident in your life. None of them know what God has planned for you. They did not create you. God did. The vision that he has designed for your life is yours alone.

You will remain stagnant and unfulfilled until such time as you stop depending upon others to assist you in your endeavors and turn your entire life completely over to God and allow him to work in and through you to bring his entire plan for your life to full fruition. I know how harsh this sounds; however, you have to strike a harmonic balance with God. There's a part of you that must take the initiative to get things done and there's a part of you that must wait for God's direction. You have to do both. I had to figure that one out for myself. People tell you to wait on God. Well, I have found, that if you do that, you might be waiting for the rest of your life. Your projects require that you use some good ole fashion common sense. I have come into your life to help you get unstuck. "Even so faith, if it hath not works, is dead, being alone." James 2:17.

As you start taking the initiative to get things done in your own life, stop worrying about how the rest of the plan is going to fall into place. Trust God and just know that it will. When God is truly ready for you to do your thing, he will bring all of it together through those individuals whom he has predetermined and selected to assist and support you in all of your endeavors in complete accordance with the will and the design that he has purposed for your life. This is precisely how God works. His ideas, his purposes and his desires will flow into and through you as his spirit and will commands.

God needs you to rest in him and trust him completely. If you look back over your life, you will be able to reflect on and see that it is him who has been guiding your every step. You are where you are today because he has kept you in spite of the circumstances in which you have found yourself engulfed.

He has literally brought you, a broken vessel, through all of it and he now stands ready to assist you in doing even greater things above and beyond

27

anything you have ever done before. All he asks in exchange is that you give him the honor, the glory, the respect, the reverence, the recognition for everything good that has happened in your life. With all due respect, everything good that has happened in your life is a direct manifestation of what God has allowed to happen in your life. Without him, you can do nothing. He has to permit and allow it to transpire. He knows your heart; he knows your will and he also knows exactly what he has blessed and empowered you to do. Allow him to use what he has given you to bless others in a pure, altruistic and magnanimous fashion.

The Ingredients of Faith

Faith characterizes incredible strength, tenacity, will, trust, belief, vision and a deep understanding of abundant living through the power, grace, mercy and anointing of God. There are a plethora of ways to examine the concept of faith, analyze it, study it, synthesize it and then reconstruct it to apply it as a means of empowering your progress.

If you build a construct of faith and allow its basic tenets to guide your life and God's will for your life, your chances of succeeding in your endeavors are imminently enhanced. Faith is about forward movement. It's fine to reflect on the past, pause for a moment, think about the mistakes you've made and still continue to make on a daily basis but you must simply never allow or permit that to keep you from moving forward.

A great friend of mine, Gene Murphy, once said, "People usually only step where the foundation is firm enough to hold. Real faith is having the ability to step out where there is no foundation and trusting God to show up and assist you in carrying out the vision he has planned for your life." Only a small fraction of individuals in our society truly understand how that works. The evidence is in Matthew 9:37 where Christ is speaking to his disciples and says, "The harvest truly is plenteous but the laborers are few." Your sustained forward movement over a long period of time is the kind of commitment that one makes to excellence that has the ability to generate results that one would never think could be possible.

This continued forward movement is all about taking repeated action. However, most are familiar with the age-old expression "Insanity is doing the same thing over and over expecting a different result." That is not the approach one should take. On the contrary, continue to take consistent action but learn from the past, look at what's working, examine what's not working, continue to get advice from others, pray fervently, continue doing those things that work best for you and simply keep honing and refining the process.

Take out the old, insert the new, acquire fresh ideas from others, grow your friends, grow your audience through positive interactions, network with others, provide people continuously with value and substantive materials in an effort to become more prolific and more effective in your endeavors and what you are doing on a daily basis. The powerful, positive habits that you develop in concert with your proactive faith are the necessary and essential ingredients that will enable you to create opportunities for great success to ensue.

Preparation Is the Key to Success

The bible is replete with stories that demonstrate the power of faith and what can be accomplished when one is motivated to do something of particular significance. Perhaps one of the most interesting and one of the most compelling stories is the story of David and Goliath.

Years ago, I think sometime in the eighties, I was in attendance at a large Amway Convention in Chicago, Illinois. I remember being surrounded by about ten thousand other people. People had traveled from all over the United States to get inspired and motivated to promote their businesses effectively. I had gone with one of my top business associates at the time, Mark Graham. He was and still is such a great friend. I distinctly remember listening to three very powerful speakers. One was the great motivational speaker, Zig Ziglar. I will always cherish his memory and his words of wisdom.

He was one of those individuals who could inspire and empower you to do just about anything. At the time, perhaps, one of his most famous books was one called, See You at the Top. I once wrote him a letter asking him to consider writing an article for a magazine called Purpose Magazine. It was published by a friend of mine by the name of Ella Coleman. He responded and let me know that he would consider that. Not long after, Mr. Zig Ziglar had a conversation with my friend, Ella Coleman and was actually featured in her magazine and wrote a couple of empowerment articles. Perhaps two of Zig Ziglar's most wise and prominent aphorisms that made a significant impact upon others in addition to his infectious enthusiasm, unique style of delivery and positive attitude were, "You can get anything in life you want if you'll just help enough other people get what they want." Zig Ziglar would share with you specific principals that you could use to move ahead in life coupled with a goal achievement strategy and then he would pause and say, "If you put these things into action, I will see you and yes, I really do mean you, at the top!" You always walked out of Zig Ziglar's seminars feeling like you could accomplish just about anything.

It's pretty amazing when I reflect on that time period in my life, who I was at that time and who I have become today. What's truly amazing was being a young man, wanting to meet this guy, getting to do that, shake his hand, chat with him on several different occasions and most importantly to have received several letters from him that are in my possession that simply encouraged me to keep doing what I am doing. How powerful is that? Zig Ziglar never got too powerful or too big to take time for the little guys. In fact, if you ever took the time to ask him what a big shot was, his response would have been, "A big shot is just a little shot that kept on shootin." Zig Ziglar understood that one of the most important concepts relevant to success in any industry lies within your ability to communicate with others effectively and to take time to interact with others regardless of their station in life. Too many people today who think of themselves as being successful simply do not understand the power of this essential principle.

The second speaker which I distinctly remember was a high-level Amway distributor by the name of Keith Belnap. Keith was a high-powered, high-energy kind of guy. Perhaps, the line I most remember from his high energy presentation was, "You don't make me happy! I make me happy!" This suffices to indicate that outside of God, you are the only person who has control over what happens in your life and how you respond to events that happen in your life. When you spend some quality time thinking about it, those are indeed very powerful words. They are words that determine your path in life. From time to time, we must pause and take note of where we are in life, what we are allowing to happen to us and consider why we are allowing others to impose their will upon our lives if such is the case.

If changes need to be made, then, perhaps we need to be the ones to make those necessary and important changes if we find ourselves stuck in a rut and have a need to get unstuck so we can start moving forward again. That means, when you are ready, it's decision time. Another one of the all time great motivational speakers, Anthony Robbins, says it this way. "It is in your moments of decision that your destiny is shaped."

The third speaker was a powerful gentleman by the name of Doug Wead. Doug told the story of David and Goliath located in 1st Samuel, chapter 17. Though I have heard that story preached from the pulpit on numerous occasions over the years, it is one of those stories that never loses its power. When you go to the Bible to read it for yourself in order to discover what precisely motivated David to challenge this gigantic philistine and what God did to prepare David for this specific encounter with Goliath, the story itself takes on an even greater significance and the strength of its message and intent resonates as an even more powerful truth in the lives of those who desire to apply its revealed wisdom to their lives.

When Doug told the story, it might amaze you to discover from your own analysis that what intrigued David most was finding out that the man who killed Goliath would reap great benefits. Ist Samuel 25. "The man who killeth him, the King will enrich him with great riches, and will give him his daughter and make his father's house free in Israel." Now, be sure to read and discover the truth for yourself. You do know how jealous people can be when they sense you are up to something, right? For David's brother, Eliab, his oldest brother's anger was kindled against him. Well, what do you do when that happens? The Bible says in that instance, 1st Samuel verse thirty. He turned from him toward another. You see, David was intent on getting to the heart of the matter and he would not stop until such time as he had done so. There is tremendous power in persistence. To put it mildly, David was a bit more than just intrigued to discover that if in fact he was the man who slew Goliath, that he would become the one who secured the hand of a princess! Wow! If that doesn't motivate you, what would? However, if one takes a deeper look at what is transpiring here, there are far more intricate details that show you the depth of David's relationship with God.

What I am asking the reader or listener to understand here is simply this. "There is no force in the world that has a greater impact than the statement of a knowledgeable person fortified by confidence and experience. An individual who knows and knows that he knows can speak with authority and conviction that has no comparison. The world makes way for the man or woman who knows where he is going."

To that end, David knew precisely what his relationship was with God. No one else knew or even had a remote inkling of what that relationship was until God was ready to reveal his power to the world through the actions that David would be taking. No one ever knows until such time as God is ready to make the world aware of his intentions. David's faith in what God can do had been fully activated before Goliath had ever entered the picture. It didn't matter that he was the youngest son of Jesse with seven older brothers.

If one needs further proof of how God had more than adequately prepared David for his upcoming encounter with Goliath, all one has to do is closely examine the scriptures for a complete and thorough explanation. Any time God prepares you, you can consider yourself prepared. Others will have nothing more to say. When David is standing before Saul, look at what scripture says.

Firstly, when Saul tries to argue with David that he is but a youth and Goliath a man of war, let's look at David's response. 1st Samuel 34. And David said unto Saul, Thy servant kept his father's sheep, and there came a lion, and a bear and took a lamb out of the flock:
Verse 35. And I went out after him and smote him and delivered it out of its mouth: and when he arose against me, I caught him by his beard and smote him and slew him.

Verse 36. Thy servant slew both the lion and the bear: and this uncircumcised philistine shall be as one of them, seeing he has defied the armies of the living God.

Verse 37. David said moreover, the Lord that delivered me out of the paw of the lion, and out of the paw of the bear, he will deliver me out of the hand of this philistine. And Saul said unto David, Go, and the Lord be with thee.

David had so much confidence and so much faith in how God was going to use him that he even knew what the outcome was going to be before the event had even transpired. In fact, it says in 1st Samuel 48, And it came to pass, when the philistine arose and drew nigh to meet David, that David hasted and ran toward the army to meet the philistine.

1st Samuel 49. And David put his hand in his bag and took thence a stone, and slang it, and smote the philistine in his forehead; and he fell upon his face to the earth.

Four things of critical importance are evident in this chapter. The first is that the full activation of your faith in God can and will produce miracles. Secondly, whatever it is that motivates and inspires you can and will be of significant value to your success. Thirdly, when God prepares you for a mission he has in mind, you can be one hundred per cent certain that you are fully prepared. Fourthly, your ability to envision success before it happens is a pure and truthful manifestation of God's will and purpose for your life. It won't be easy but all you have to do to get to the point where you are able to perform at your highest level of excellence is to be consistently relentless in your pursuit of it.

When I began my professional teaching career in the fall of 1973, one of my favorite authors, Dr. Robert Schuller, also had a TV program called "The Hour of Power". His church was situated in Garden Grove, California. He had developed a coin that I used to carry in my pocket. It was called "The possibility Thinker's Creed" and it went like this. "When faced with a mountain, I will not quit. I will keep on striving until I climb over, find a pass through, tunnel underneath or stay right there and turn the mountain into a goldmine with God's help." I found that particular expression pretty powerful in my life at that time. It still is today along with many others positive expressions, aphorisms and quotes that I have since added to my storehouse of knowledge for inspiration and motivation that fuels your determination to keep moving forward in life.

What is the Goliath or mountain in your life that you need to overcome? How will you go about attacking your adversary? This Goliath or mountain that I am referring to is merely a metaphor that stands between you and the dream that God desires you to birth into existence and manifest into life through you. Every experience that you have brings you closer to the destiny you were designed to fulfill. It is exactly as William Jennings Bryan has said, "Destiny is not a matter of chance. It is a matter of choice. It is not a thing to be hoped for, it is a thing to be achieved. In 2nd Timothy 1:7, the Bible states, "For God hath not given us the spirit of fear; but of power, and of love, and of a sound mind."

Just knowing that and just knowing that God has already prepared and purposed you for great and amazing things contains a seed that has the power to release an even more equivalent or greater benefit.

Spiritual Wisdom

The nature of God's thinking,
Is the muse of mental health;
Herein lies the secret,
Of the treasure trove of wealth.

The more one comes to understand,
The essence of his love;
The more one seeks to do his will,
With guidance from above.

Sometimes life's so tumultuous,
It seems that all is lost;
But then we're oft reminded,
God paid the total cost.

So when the mountains seem so steep,
And valleys spew despair;
Is when God touches base with you,
To demonstrate his care.

No matter what the world may say,
Or what most others do;
As long as you maintain your faith,
God's love will see you through.

The branch cannot bear fruit itself,
It hangs there on the limb;
If thou desirest good success,
You must abide in him.

All blessings are bestowed from God,
His truth will set you free;
Through his love you can become,
The best that you can be.

Momentum

Momentum is a powerful thing,
In what you choose to do;
You motivate, you contemplate,
And then you follow through.

The smoothness of transition,
On the quest which you embark;
Brings some lofty compensation,
When you ignite that inner spark.

The awesome gift of spectacle,
The softness of the breeze;
Stirs the scent inside your nostrils,
As it filters through the trees.

The flow of maturation,
Brings the bliss of true compense;
And your traction on the surface,
Helps you scale the picket fence.

You understand the mission,
As a team or all alone;
And you cannot feel the pressure,
When you're locked into the zone.

The awesome gift of talent,
It's the thing that conquers all;
And you can feel the surge of energy,
When you simply heed the call.

The power of momentum,
And the instinctive path you choose;
Builds tremendous confidence,
It makes it hard to lose.

The attitude of gratitude,
Will rise above a balk;
And the prize will then be handed,
To the one who walks his talk.

Power

And Jesus came and spake unto them saying, "All power is given unto me in heaven and in earth. Matthew 28:18. All power originates from God. "The eyes of the Lord range throughout the earth to strengthen those whose hearts are fully committed to him. 2nd Chronicles 16:9. Strength is power.

From whence does it come? "I will look to the hills, from whence cometh my help. My help cometh from the Lord, which made heaven and earth. Psalm 121: 1-2. God has no limitations; therefore, his power is unlimited. Allow your mind to concentrate and fixate on that for just a moment. When you do, you will be able to immediately be able to acknowledge or give deference to an incredible, spiritual being who stood outside of time itself and created it. It is truly a most uncanny paradox. Another way of looking at it is to simply say, God started start. Take a moment if you will to just wrap your mind around that. God's power has unlimited capabilities and he can imbue you with an abundance of it as he deems it necessary and appropriate.

For all intents and purposes, this chapter forms an acronym for power and observes just five of its primary attributes. These attributes or characteristics of power are indeed formidable. The more clearly you can delineate and refine these substantive qualities, the more effective power becomes as you utilize it in your own life.

The purpose for which God has framed you can easily become the driving force behind your power. What is the rationale for what it is that a person finds himself doing? What specific habits drive him or her to repeat an action over and over? Aristotle once said, "Habits are what we repeatedly do." It can be this startling discovery that enables an individual to achieve his highest and most noble aspirations. The dormant and untapped reservoirs and capabilities of the human mind and heart must, can and will be driven by a dominant, formidable and uniquely designed purpose. Therein lies the first step in achieving ultimate power. The more clearly delineated and refined that purpose is, the more powerful and dominant it becomes.

There's a logical pattern that creates the energy flow that makes the achievement of power possible. It is this. Once you have identified your purpose and it's very possible that you might have more than one, it becomes a matter of how obedient you are going to be to the achievement of that ultimate purpose that results in power. How committed are you to the process? What if it's going to take you years to develop the skills, the abilities, the talents and the gifts you must have? Will you make the sacrifice? Will you put in the time, energy and the effort that is required that will enable you to achieve your purposeful and powerful objective once you have discovered it?

In other words, you must be obedient to the spiritual force that is driving you to your destined encounter. It is exactly as the Bible says, "But without faith, it is impossible to please him. For he that cometh to God must believe that he is and that he is a rewarder of those who diligently seek him." Hebrews 11:6

Your destiny lies solely in your own hands. It is you who must take the responsibility of dribbling the ball the length of the court and slam dunking it when you arrive at the other end. The power to do so is literally in your hands. What are you going to do with it? It is this level of commitment and obedience that sets you apart from every other being on the planet. Your obedience and your willingness to acknowledge its intrinsic merit is your golden ticket to the achievement of ultimate success. Be obedient. Stay the course. "And let us not be weary in well doing: for in due season we shall reap if we faint not." Galatians 5:9

Staying the course requires tremendous wisdom and wisdom comes through experience, tenaciousness, informed decision-making, trial and error, repeatedly doing things over and over and over that do not work, banging your head against the wall, allowing bad habits to dominate, control and consume your efforts as you submit to your fancies and whims in wasting your time by succumbing to your own false sense of self and erroneous passions. Have I hit a nerve yet? Good! I am also guilty as charged. This means you're on the right track. It's called living. It means you understand. Life is called being a human being and being swayed by all of those things that appeal to your vanity. The more time you spend chasing those things that are not pertinent and meaningful to your true endeavors, the longer it will take you to accomplish your real life goals. If you truly want to be successful, you have to continually ask God for direction, meaning and purpose in your life and have faith in knowing that he will be there to assist you in your endeavors. "Lo, I am with you always even unto the the end of the world." Matthew 28:20.

When these temptations of which I speak begin to fall away from you, only then will the more effective you emerge to pursue your most meaningful and most impactful goals and dreams. You will know that you are on the right track because every fiber of your being will be on fire for the direction in which you are headed. There won't be any second guessing. You will know.

It is a very powerful thing that transpires deep within your soul. Thus, when your wisest self emerges to take control of your dominant thinking over where you are headed in life, it is because you have learned to apply what you know in the proper way. This is what wisdom is. It contains the gift of discernment and the right application of knowledge.

The sudden alacrity that encompasses your being is brought about by the genuine quality of exuberance that serves as the guiding force propelling you forward in search of the same destiny that is seeking you. That genuine power that is seeking you is exactly what Ralph Waldo Emerson has stated in his powerful quote, "Nothing great was ever accomplished without enthusiasm." It is the one common denominator that can be found in all matters that are relevant to the further advancement and refinement of significant human achievement. Consistency is key to the parabolic rise of both spiritual and human significance and meaning.

The last principle that unleashes the fullness of pure, unadulterated power is its inevitable endurance and sustainability hidden in the impenetrable armor of resilience and perseverance. Life is replete with millions of stories of those individuals who've encountered nothing but obstacles in their way on their own individual paths to greatness. It has always been and always will be the greatest satisfaction of all when you're the one who rises to the very top of your profession with your arms folded knowing that it mattered not what others thought about your lot in life. The only thing that mattered was what you believed and thought. This in the end is what proved to be the dominating thought-factor in the life of your most distinguished achievement. It was Emerson once again who said, "Nothing is at last sacred but the integrity of your own mind."

Real power consists of many, many things but perhaps five of its most notable attributes are purpose, obedience, wisdom, exuberance and resilience. (POWER). It is this kind of insight, this kind of stubborn tenacity and this kind of consistent consistency formulated, perpetuated and used to altruistically push others to maximize their full potential that stirs the hearts, minds and souls of those who are destined to be the true difference-makers in our society. Peace be to you whose minds are set to enhance, inspire and improve the quality of life for others through faith in Jesus Christ and that not of yourselves lest any man should boast.

It is written in Philippians, "Brethern, I count not myself to have apprehended: but this one thing I do, forgetting those things which are behind, and reaching forth unto those things which are before, I press toward the mark for the prize of the high calling in Christ Jesus. Philippians 3:13-14.

Power

Power is ubiquitous,
Designed to conquer all;
As you recognize the treasure,
So embedded in your call;

As you understand your purpose,
And the gift you have to give;
You will comprehend its value,
Teaching others how to live.

Your obedience to stay,
That rocky road or course;
Will put on full display,
Your character of force.

True wisdom is revealed,
In decisions that you make;
Your choices play a factor,
In whatever role you take.

Exuberance is critical,
For one so truly blessed;
It's the substance of the soul,
That engenders great success.

Resilience is the master key,
Empowering you to win;
When you fall down in the trenches,
You must rise up once again.

In the end, it's not the gold,
When the race of life is won;
The thing that matters most,
Is the person you've become.

The Phenomenal Encourager

God is the phenomenal encourager. It is evident through John 3:16. "For God so loved the world that he gave his only begotten son that whosoever believeth in him should not perish but have everlasting life." This was such an incredible thing for the ultimate spiritual being to do.

When Jesus himself speaks to his disciples in John 14: 1-3, he further validates and supports this great and inevitable truth by his direct statement to them when he says, "Let not your hearts be troubled: ye believe in God, believe also in me. In my father's house are many mansions: If it were not so, I would have told you. And if I go to prepare a place for you, I will come again, and receive you unto myself; that where I am, there ye may be also." Jesus was encouraging them to increase their faith in him. When one thinks of the triune God or the Holy Trinity, the father, the son and the Holy Spirit, Jesus wanted them to know and understand that the Holy Deity for the concept of God works in perfect unity to resolve the problems of the world.

The more solid and steadfast our relationship is with him, the more effective we can be in our relationship with others. Christ knows that the more we understand and acknowledge our relationship with him, the more credibility we will have in spreading the gospel of Jesus Christ. He goes so far as to say in John 15:4 "Abide in me, and I in you. As the branch cannot bear fruit of itself except it abide in the vine, neither can you, unless you abide in me." What a powerful example and analogy this is for those who are looking to achieve outstanding results in this world as a means of leading people to Christ. As you move forward in life, it becomes incumbent upon you to determine where you are in your personal walk with him. This can play a significant role in your future success as well as your self-preservation. God can and will protect those that he loves.

Those who are looking for success must understand and acknowledge the power of God and his word. Indeed, the word of

God is so powerful. In order to achieve even worldly success, God illustrates how people must think and act in relationship to the acquisition of their desires. His desire is for you to make sure that your priorities are in order. This is why he states in Matthew 6:33, "But seek ye first the kingdom of heaven and his righteousness; and all these things shall be added unto you." To ascertain the full scope of this scriptural passage, make sure you read the entire chapter for yourself. I have read it many times and it is indeed a very powerful one.

The German Philosopher, Johann Wolfgang Von Goethe once said, "Whatever you can do or dream you can, begin it. Boldness has genius, power and magic in it." As has been stated earlier in this text, God has endowed you with amazing talents, skills, abilities, gifts and along with that, provides you with many opportunities to utilize them fully. What are you doing about that?

It has often been stated on many occasions that success occurs where preparation and opportunity meet. The Bible provides you with profound support in your endeavors. In Philippians 4:13, apostle Paul writes, "I can do all things through Christ which strengtheneth me." A deep-rooted belief in Jesus Christ and his ability to empower you lends credence to the positive impact Christ can and will have in your life.

You cannot go into the presence of God with a half-hearted attitude. Prayer is one of the most powerful ways in which you can communicate with God. If there is something you truly desire, remember what Goethe said about being bold. Go boldly to the throne of grace. Ask with a firmness in attitude, disposition, commitment that most do not. In James 5:16, the Bible states that "The effectual, fervent prayer of a righteous man availeth much." Those aren't just mere words. Show God through your words, your actions and your deeds how strong your desires are. Matthew 7:7 tells you specifically how God responds to those true believers who demonstrate persistence. "Ask and ye shall receive, seek and ye shall find, knock and it shall be opened unto you." Again, these are powerful, powerful words, are they not? The real question is this. How seriously do you take them?

The Holy Bible is not just a collection of inspirational and motivational writings that was assembled by a group of individuals, more importantly it is the pure, unadulterated living word of God that quickens your spirit (makes it alive). True believers who enter the presence of God through his holy word and through his son Jesus Christ can feel that and when you are affected by that kind of power, eventually, something powerful and magnificent happens. You can count on it.

This powerful and revealing truth is further validated by Mark 9:23. Jesus said unto him, "If thou canst believe, all things are possible to him that believeth." Do you know what Jesus is actually doing here? He is asking you a simple question. The question really is, "Where is your faith?" He also uses the conditional word "If" coupled with (believe).

He wants to know whether or not you truly believe in the Son, the Father and the Holy Spirit. This is precisely why the Bible states that "Without faith, it is impossible to please him. You simply must activate your faith. Once God has the assurance that he can trust you to do his will and he knows for a fact that you believe in the power that he has to accomplish anything, it is "game over." From that point forward, he can work with and through you. I haven't met anyone yet who is capable of placing a limitation on what God can do or how he can use you in a meritorious way. He has purposed you for great and amazing things. It's not your job to know exactly how or when it's going to happen. The real test lies in the fact that your faith just has to be strong enough to know that it will.

The Phenomenal Encourager

Staring into failure's face,
Oh what a daunting task;
Especially when the odds are placed,
And you are pegged as last.

Hope appears most fleeting,
As the shades of night roll in;
It seems there's no use thinking,
There's a chance you still can win.

And yet that voice inside of you,
That stirs your heart and soul;
Whispers in your listening ear,
Relinquish not your goal.

Though failure is a part of life,
Affecting young and old;
The way you handle setbacks,
Determines how you roll.

Encouragement is the lifeline,
In a sea of struggling souls;
Confronted by life's failures,
And a mounting list of woes.

The phenomenal encourager,
Shows up when hope is lost;
And reaches out to take your hand,
For he has borne the cross.

Failure is not final,
And the God that lives within;
Is greater than the worldly gods,
With Him, you always win.

Endurance

It was our first day back in church on May 31st of 2020 amid the outbreak of the Covid-19 pandemic that spread around the world usurping the lives of millions of international and United States citizens. This dreaded airborne pathogenic upper respiratory infection has been devastating. Not since the pandemic of 1918 have we borne witness to anything of this magnitude. As of August 21st, 2022 the coronavirus death toll stood at a staggering 6, 470,000 and 926 people. I have had it twice so far, my wife, Debbie has had it once. The vaccinations and boosters are making an awesome difference in curbing the number of deaths. We are both so thankful to still be here. So far, God has seen fit to bless us and to keep our families safe. We are indebted to him for that. To God be the glory. He doesn't have to do it, but he does. This devastating plague provides us with just one more opportunity to illustrate the power of God's grace and mercy. Our families are still here and we are indeed most thankful for that. Many, many other families are much less fortunate.

I attend Pleasant Green Baptist Church in Portsmouth, Ohio. We have a mask policy in place to slow down the spread of the Coronavirus. A lot of folks are attending church online through Facebook, google links, YouTube and through the effective utilization of other social media platforms. It's safer that way. The coronavirus has changed the way we live and conduct business for now. People are far more cautious than they have ever been and they are right to be so. Now is not the time to be careless. Using good common sense can increase an individual's longevity in this world.

At any rate, I made it to church on the morning of May 31 of 2020. And one of our associate ministers, Joe Green was set to deliver the morning message. None of us alive who were in the church at that time had ever witnessed such a life-threatening disease as the coronavirus pandemic. Joe's message was most timely. He spoke directly from 2nd Timothy, Chapter 2 verses 1-5.

1. Thou therefore, my son, be strong in the grace that is in Christ Jesus.

2. And the things that thou hast heard of me among many witnesses, the same commit thou to faithful men, who shall be able to teach others also.

3. Thou therefore endure hardness, as a good soldier of Jesus Christ.

4. No man that warreth entangleth himself with the affairs of this life; that he may please him who hath chosen him to be a soldier.

5. And if a man strive for masteries, yet is he not crowned, except he strive lawfully.

It was indeed a most revelatory and timely message for both members of the congregation as well as the general population. His message for those who desire to possess a success-oriented mentality focused on the power hidden in endurance.

Joe preached and the majority of us in the sanctuary took heed as he laid out what God had placed upon his heart. He defined endurance as the ability to endure hardship or adversity. He went on to articulate clearly and matter-of-factly that "whenever you face hardship, stress or pain, you have a tendency to quit." He moved on with his commentary. "Are you a warrior or a soldier?" He begged the question. As minister, Joe Greene, revealed what God had placed on his heart, he gave us three specific and powerful concepts to place in our spirits.

1. Prepare to deal effectively with resistance over time by making yourself strong. In other words, don't just travel the flat roads. Put some hills in your journey. Prepare yourself for the obstacles you have to overcome. Understand that you didn't just start out on this journey; you were chosen for it. You must understand that

endurance is developed through stress. God is favoring you. Be grateful you are receiving and thank God.

2. The second most powerful concept that Minister Greene focused on was your ability to develop the mindset of a soldier. Are you equipped and prepared for battle? In other words, you have to be if your desire and your passion is to win. How much effort are you willing to put forth in order to determine how effective you are going to be as a leader or to get through whatever it is you are going through? You have to toughen yourself up in order to be successful. And you can't just be a soldier; you have to be a good soldier. Not all soldiers make it through the process. Many of them are weeded out in basic training. Only the strong survive. That's the kind of soldier you have to be.

In order to be successful in any endeavor, you have to be willing to endure a lot. My family has been very blessed over the years. My first wife, Shannon L. Lawson studied sedulously and completed all the requirements for the acquisition of her doctoral degree in communications. My second wife, Debbie Lawson received her vocational degree and worked for 24 years at the Dallas Fort Worth Airport in Dallas, Texas before moving on to Auto Nation for another 15 years. "It takes guts to leave the ruts."

When my oldest son, Robert L. Lawson Jr. was still in high school, he became a member of the ROTC program (Reserve Officers Training Corp). My second son, James Allen Lawson received his baccalaureate with a major in Computer Information Systems and a minor in Finance. He is putting both to use in a phenomenal way and he has this drive to acquire new information and then use it effectively.

My youngest son, Michael Emerson Lawson, went on to obtain his baccalaureate degree before enlisting in the

Navy. I drove to Illinois to watch him graduate from basic training. Mike always gave me updates on what he was doing, He was first in his company in the one and one- half mile run and had conditioned his body to do one hundred pushups all in one set. I personally felt that this was an amazing accomplishment.

When he completed his basic training, he was sent to Pensacola, Florida and on from there to the state of Washington and is now in San Diego, California where he has resided for the past couple of years. He has finished with the next phase of his career. During the latter part of 2022, Mike received an honorable discharge from the Navy. I am so very proud of him and the rest of my family members. I have tremendous admiration for their grit, determination and persistence in staying the course, learning from their experiences and understanding that in order to achieve the basics in life, you must be willing to endure.

James Allen, the English essayist once said, "The strength of the effort is the measure of the result." According to Minister Joe Greene, you have to develop a warrior's mentality in order to survive. Understand that Jesus Christ is the manifestation of grace and his grace is sufficient for all of us and can take us through anything that we think we might not be able to get through. Minister Joe Greene says, "You will always be trapped until you become strong of yourself." What lies within the integrity of your own mind is where the change must occur in order for it to move from an internal process to an outward manifestation.

The pandemic has presented all of us with an amazing opportunity for some serious soul-searching and deep, reflective thought even about the very air we breathe in and out of our lungs on a daily basis. Today, life is here but tomorrow in the twinkling of an eye, it can all be gone. Oh, how fragile, temporal and ephemeral this earthly life is. Even though that has always been the case, the pandemic has certainly heightened our awareness to such an in-your-face reality.

What are our most powerful goals and aspirations? Why have we not achieved them yet? What is holding us back? In James Allen's powerful treatise, As a Man Thinketh, he makes a powerful statement. "You can be as small as your controlling desire or as great as your dominant aspiration." Perhaps the answer to what is holding you back lies in the third and final revelation reflected in Minister Green's powerful message.

3. "Be careful what you entangle yourself with." In other words, what must you let go of in order to move forward.? In the book of James in the New Testament, when God speaks through James in chapter one, he makes the path towards success very clear indeed. Verse 6 "But let him ask in faith, nothing wavering. For he that wavereth is like a wave of the sea driven with the wind and tossed." Verse 7 "For let not that man think that he shall receive anything of the Lord." Verse 8 "A double-minded man is unstable in all his ways.

If you are ever to achieve the objectives you are bent on achieving in life, God needs and requires your complete and total focus. Verse 12 "Blessed is the man that endureth temptation: for when he is tried, he shall receive the crown of life, which the Lord hath promised to them that love him."

We can't blame God for our shortcomings. We have to grow through our weaknesses and become better people as a result of having grown. Verse 13 "Let no man say when he is tempted, I am tempted by God: For God cannot be tempted with evil, neither tempteth he any man." Verse 14. "But every man is tempted when he is drawn away of his own lust and enticed."

Even though temptation abounds on every hand, God's word remains powerful and illustrates the beauty that awaits those who are able to activate and maintain the faith that God requires while at the same time resisting temptation. Verse 17. "Every good gift and every perfect gift is from above, and cometh down from the father of lights, with whom is no variableness, neither shadow or turning."

In the heart of his sermon, Minister Green points out the following: "A soldier doesn't have time to entangle himself with a ton of trouble." He referenced a book by Angela Duckworth, entitled *Grit.* He related a story from her book that begs to be repeated here. Whatever it is that you do, be passionate about it and have purpose. The story he shared was this. "When the cadets come in, their hours are occupied from 6:OO a.m. until 1O:OO p.m." If your hours are filled, you have no time for distractions!!! I heard that!!! For me, that was one of those wow! Moments. A "wow" moment is one of those moments that my friend, Mike Jennings talks about. Mike is a former instructor at Georgetown Jr.-Sr. High School where he taught for 15 years but has now transitioned into becoming a highly successful real estate agent. He recently captured one of his agency's top sales awards called, "The Rising Star Award." Mike's daughter, Harper, is the love of his life and every moment he spends with her is a "Wow" moment whether it's out on the banks fishing, swimming in the pool or taking a short trip to the dairy queen.

You have to pick and choose what you consider those "wow" moments for you and capture the essence and beauty of each one of them while there is yet time. Wow!!! No plan, no passion and no purpose gets you nowhere! Entangled means to be woven together. If it's not good, get away from it. Perhaps you cannot do it alone but with God's help, you can. Minister Joe Greene reminded us with his "nugget of wisdom" at the very close of his powerful message. "Always remember who you are, where you came from and what your spiritual heritage is."

Your humility and your acknowledgement of the God-power that resides in you will be the very thing that catapults you into the realm of success far beyond anything your limited mind can dream or imagine. After all, it was God himself who said, "Your ways are not my ways and your thoughts are not my thoughts. Can you imagine what it must be like to have perfect thought?

ENDURANCE

When you're stressed beyond your limits,
And your mind is racked with pain;
And the storms of life are raging,
And the sky is filled with rain.

Understand you're on a mission,
Being built for what to do;
And no one here has any thought,
Of what you're going through.

As you prepare for strong resistance,
And the pressures start to mount;
Simply know that God is with you,
His presence reigns throughout the count.

Endurance is the tree of life,
That conquers every foe;
Submitting not to challenges,
Nor recognizing woe.

The things that you have mastered,
By how well you have prepared;
Have built your mind and body,
Far beyond what most have dared.

Your mind is more than conqueror,
Withstands the test of time;
Knows exactly what to do,
When lives are on the line.

You are the marching soldier,
This is the path you trod;
You were chosen for this mission,
And today you walk with God.

Moving Forward in Faith

The word "faith" in the English – language edition of the New Testament is interchangeable with the Greek word {pistis} – which is also translated as "belief," "faithfulness" or "trust". Christianity encompasses various views regarding the nature of faith. Many believe that true faith results in good works. Others believe that while faith in Jesus Christ brings eternal life, it does not necessarily result in good works. The thief on the cross is often used as an example although he was granted eternal life through the grace and mercy of Jesus Christ. The key here is that he repented of his sins as he hung there on the cross. Christ recognized the sincerity of his heart in that moment and said, "Thou shalt this very day be in paradise with me." Who wouldn't want to serve a God who possesses that kind of redemption power? God's entire purpose for coming here through the manifestation of his son, Jesus Christ, was to restore man unto himself in the great chain of being. Think about it. You have more than likely lived an entire crime-filled life filled with hatred, strife and have inflicted unnecessary pain on others and in that moment, Christ has the heart to forgive you of your sins.

Neither did Saul do good works before he became Paul, after being struck blind on the road to Damascus. Neither of these men were model Christians, were they? And yet, it was God's grace that saved them in the end. God's ability to do whatever he wants speaks to the fact that he is transcendent. He is above all things. His will is sovereign.

Regardless of which approach an individual considers about faith, all can agree that it is perfectly aligned with the ideals and examples of the life that Jesus lived. He left no one behind and he guided his closest followers not merely by words but by his very actions and deeds. Any time Christ ministered to others, he purposely made sure that he left no one behind. Scripture validates his every move and justifies his every action. Jesus Christ walked and talked his incredible and amazing leadership style and modeled it for us all the way to the end of his life and after that. What an almighty God we serve. If the world evaluated his behavior, oh what a different place in which we would live.

In the book of Luke, chapter 8, verse 23, Jesus enters a ship with his disciples. The Bible tells us what happened. "But as they sailed, he fell asleep: and there came down a storm of wind on the lake; and they were filled with water and were in jeopardy." Verse 24 "And they came to him, and awoke him, saying, Master, master, we perish. Then he arose, and rebuked the wind and the raging of the water: and they ceased and there was a calm. Verse 25 "And he said unto them, Where is your faith? And they being afraid wondered, saying one to another, what manner of man is this: for he commanded even the winds and water, and they obey him.

Jesus was always in teaching mode through his words, actions and deeds. Not only did he want his disciples to hear and see what he was doing, he wanted them to be able to take the concept of faith and individually apply it to their lives so they could use this incredible super power to benefit others. How amazing and incredible is that?

In the 17th chapter of Matthew, a certain man approached the Lord. He wanted the Lord to have mercy on his son. His son's spirit was vexed and he was falling all over the place. He explained to the Lord that his disciples could not help him as they could not cure him. In verse 2, Jesus explains to them why they were not successful. Listen to and ponder his words. And Jesus said unto them, "Because of your unbelief: for verily I say unto you, If ye have faith as a grain of mustard seed, ye shall say unto this mountain, Remove hence to yonder place; and it shall remove; and nothing shall be impossible to you."

The Christian sees the mystery of God and his grace and seeks to know and become obedient to God. To a Christian, faith is not static but causes one to learn more of God and to grow. Christian faith has its origin in God. In his book, Risking, Dr. David Viscott says, "If your life is ever going to get better, you have to take chances." That statement makes a ton of sense in the grand scheme of things. Sometimes just good old-fashioned common sense will help you to go farther in life than you ever thought you could. It's not always about rocket science or being the sharpest tool in the shed. Sometimes, it's just about understanding the basics of success and timing. Sometimes, it's about the old styles and adages that have shaped and molded who we are and have become over the years. For example, "You can't steal second base by keeping your foot on first." Yes, we must at times be willing to step out, be bold, build relationships with others and try some things that have never been tried before. Change is difficult for a lot of people because we fall in love with our comfort zones. Growing requires a certain amount of uncertainty and yet change is one of the things we can depend on. Whether we like it or not, it's going to happen.

I once saw an expression on a beautiful card that is right in line with the thinking of David Viscott. It was written by Ellen Cuomo. Here it is. "Faith is risking what is for what is yet to be. It is taking small steps knowing that they lead to bigger ones. Faith is holding on when you want to let go. It is letting go when you want to hold on. Faith is looking beyond what is and trusting for what will be. It is the presence of light in darkness and the presence of God in all."

We are living in the midst of uncertain times and it is during these times that we must activate our faith, place our trust in God, pray diligently and allow him to lead, direct and guide our paths into truth and righteousness. His will, his way, his words and his wisdom will always be incredibly beneficial and masterfully significant to all that we think, say and do.

MOVING FORWARD IN FAITH

Faith can move a mountain,
When it's focused on a deed;
As it concentrates its power,
Like a planted mustard seed.

Faith will conquer fear,
And put failure in its place;
As you press on to the mark,
To complete life's rugged race.

The stronger you believe,
In your internal gift;
The more you'll strive to act,
To give a soul a lift.

Faith engenders hope,
And it punctures deep despair;
It builds intrepid courage,
And it faces down the dare.

The more you move with faith,
The more you're poised to win;
Against tremendous odds,
You'll rise up once again.

The challenges you face,
Were meant to test your will;
To strengthen your resolve,
And hone your every skill.

Faith banishes all doubt,
It resurrects the gleam;
It clears the path in front of you,
So you can live the dream.

Leadership, Faith and Transformation

Leadership and faith are inextricably bound together. That powerful connection eventually leads to transformation. Though we may not reach it, Christ set the ultimate standard for all of us to follow. He hit the mark of perfection which is something for which we can all strive. He was without sin. Years ago, I attended an empowerment seminar held by Tony Robbins in Cincinnati, Ohio. Tony shared a powerful definition of leadership. What he said was this. "Leadership is the power to influence behavior." It is indeed a most succinct definition of leadership and certainly, a number of the experts I have read like Dr. Stephen Covey, Warren Bennis, Peter Drucker and Henriette Ann Clauser will all provide you with deep and fascinating insights into leadership. In fact, leadership has many, many dimensions, attributes and characteristics but arguably, it is Jesus Christ who emerges as the historical figure and Lord and Savior whose influence on the lives of others makes any comparison to his style, his works and his impact on the lives of others remarkably inferior to his words, his works, his ways and his wisdom. As you search and review the scriptures, you will reach that conclusion yourself. The deeper God's word seeps into your heart, the more you will want to do his will for your life.

Leadership and faith are wrought or forged in the valley of hard work. A muscle does not become strong in and of itself. It requires repeated exercise. I heard a minister say in a sermon once years ago, "There can be no mountain if there are no valleys." Do these words make sense to you? God's definition of leadership and his implementation of faith through his son Jesus Christ is where real transformation occurs. Real leadership only comes when you take God at his word, trust him completely and allow his spirit to flow through you.

It cannot be forced. You simply must be patient and wait on God to deliver his perfect will and intent to your mind. This is when your mind is quickened {made alive} and then God can fill your soul with his direction, meaning, will and purpose for your life. In order for you to fully understand and implement the concepts and ideas contained in leadership, faith and the power of transformation that is to occur in your life, you have to move self completely out of the way. You must empty yourself of the ideas inherent in your own mind and allow God to use your experiences, your background and what you are learning now. The secret lies in how he has prepared you thus far and where your walk currently lies with him now. This is what is creating and manifesting the destiny you are designed to fulfill.

As you move forward, God will reveal his spirit and intent to your mind. You simply have to clear your mind, trust him completely and allow him to work through you. God tells you in Revelations 3:2O. "Behold, I stand at the door and knock: If any man hear my voice, and open the door, I will come in to him, and will sup with him, and he with me."

These words that I am writing now are as much for me as they are for you. I'm putting this in a context that I can understand and explain so that I can get my point across to you in order that you may incorporate this methodology concerning leadership, faith and transformation into your own life.

There is an incredible and purposeful correlation between faith and leadership. Without leadership, faith is meaningless. Earlier, when you read the story about Jesus asleep on the ship and the storms came, all the disciples were sore afraid until Jesus work up and showed them what to do. Another facet of leadership is evident in that passage. Leadership and faith work when you do. Faith is belief through demonstrated action and leadership is all about building effective relationships with others while taking the initiative to get things done. All Jesus said was, "Peace be still." And the disciples marveled that both the winds and the sea obeyed him. This is a teachable moment. All Jesus was trying to do was to get his disciples to understand how powerful they already were. In other words, how strong is your belief level in what God is telling you to do? The real secret of your success lies in your level of belief in God, in yourself and in what God is telling you to do. It is time for you to take action.

God constantly equips you for the work he plans for you to do by making sure that you acquire the tools you need through past experiences, education and situational events. Your attitude and your disposition towards life also play an instrumental role in determining your effectiveness as a leader. Through prayer, fasting, and study God's intentionality for your life becomes more evident. This is how he empowers you to do his will.

I'm going to take the time to revisit just a few of the concepts and ideas that I've written about in a few of my other books because of their relevance and significance here. I'm doing it because these ideas have become staples in my life. I already know how powerful they are because of their effectiveness in my own life. When you discover something that you know works, you want to share it with others so that they can have the same opportunities to implement those things into their lives as you did in yours.

Years ago, I read a powerful book by Dr. David Schwartz. The book was entitled,
The Magic of Thinking Big. I may not remember a lot from that book but there were three words I saw that literally changed my life forever. Here they are. Action cures fear. Here's the deal. Later on in life, I would have that powerful truth further validated when I read these powerful words by Eleanor Roosevelt. "You gain strength, you gain courage and you gain confidence by every experience in which you step up to look fear in the face. You must literally learn to do the things you think you cannot do." From a leadership perspective, how powerful is that? If you're looking for further validation to solidify these great truths in your mind, look no further than another powerful book I read years ago, *Think and Grow Rich* by Napoleon Hill. The book has created many millionaires many times over because certain individuals picked up the book, read it and took the time to apply the timeless principles they found written there to their own lives. Perhaps the most powerful statement of all in Napoleon Hill's book was this

one. "Whatever the mind can conceive and believe, it can achieve."

Christ led by example and his faith in his Holy Father was paramount to everything else. His leadership style coupled with his level of faith made everything he did, touch or talk about transformative. In fact, Christ was the embodiment and manifestation of perfect faith. His level of belief in the power with which God endowed him was so great and so remarkably profound that there was literally nothing that he could not accomplish. The only reason why he lay down to die was because he was being obedient to his father's holy will for the sake of man's redemption. In John 15:13, Jesus says, "Greater love hath no man than this, that a man lay down his life for his friends." In some ways, Jesus was already foreshadowing what was eventually going to happen before it did. He knew what was coming and what he had to do. Fortunately, though, that was not the end of the story. Jesus was crucified, he died, he was placed in a tomb but on the 3rd day
, he was resurrected. In Matthew 28:18 it tells us what happened. "And Jesus came and spake unto them, saying, All power is given unto me in heaven and in earth."

The Power of Transformation

The power of transformation,
Comes from the touch of God;
He infiltrates the human soul,
Assembled from the sod.

The more you utilize your skills,
From digging down and deep,
You'll understand that what you sow's
Exactly what you'll reap.

The change must come from deep within,
To spread hope far and wide;
It's destined to evoke a trust,
That fills a soul with pride.

Transformation thus requires,
A bold intrepid plan;
Sustained with solid action,
And a will that knows it can.

Every day there are distractions,
That will seek to wrest control;
Diverting all your energy,
To thwart a worthy goal.

Just remember you're the captain,
You're in charge of where you steer;
And the vision in your head,
Must be the one that's crystal clear.

So let no thing deter you,
No matter where you roam;
It's your final transformation,
That will drive your point home.

A great friend of mine by the name of Julius Cartwright says it this way. "If you are fulfilled, you are probably resting too much. Work is God's pathway to a satisfying, meaningful existence. Stop wondering and start looking inside for one of the many talents that you have. I've heard of Monday through Sunday but I've never heard of some day. It all begins in your mind. What you give power to has power over you if you allow it."

"God has already put a lot of time into you. When you put a little time back into God through prayer, meditation and study, that investment will always pay off. That's why when we start our day out reflecting on all the things we have to be thankful for, we have a much more rewarding day. It takes courage to grow up and turn out to be who you really are."

God's Plan and Purpose

God's plan and purpose for your life,
These are the things you need to know;
How much you can accomplish,
And how far you need to go.

Understand the main connection,
Through your prayers and your trust;
The faith of your conviction,
Becomes the force behind your thrust.

So you build in total confidence,
Because you feel the inner light;
Of the spiritual sagacity,
All by faith and none by sight.

Find your strength within your weakness,
Turn your plans to solid gold;
Understand your true propensity,
Lies inside the hand you hold.

They stretched him high, they hung him wide,
He bled and died on calvary's cross;
But in the end, he rose again,
So every soul would not be lost.

He reigns above and in your heart,
Through all the world's travails and pain;
He understands your role, your part,
All victory lies in Jesus' name.

As you contemplate the nature,
Of the awesome God above;
He's not the author of confusion,
He's the father of true love.

God Knows Best

Not that long ago, I was talking with one of my friends who lives in southern California. His name is Tony Murphy. When Tony was involved in pursuing his undergraduate degree at Marshall University in Huntington, West Virginia, that at a time when he was confronted with a particular challenge that one of his amazing friends, Barbara Frye, gave him a poem that was written by the famous Helen Steiner Rice. That particular poem had a very positive impact upon Tony because it changed his perspective on what was happening in his life at that time and encouraged him to keep moving forward.

Tony, his brother Gene, Greg, Franklin and all the Murphys I know are extremely successful individuals and I am absolutely thrilled to call them friends. If you are supposed to be known by the company you keep and your success can be measured by those who are members of your inner circle, then, I don't mind telling you that I have surrounded myself with some of the best friends and best minds ever. I personally found the poem Tony shared with me significantly valuable as well as deeply insightful. Here it is. God Knows Best by Helen Steiner Rice.

GOD KNOWS BEST

Our father knows what's best for us,
So why should we complain;
We always want the sunshine,
But we know there must be rain.

We love the sound of laughter,
And the merriment of cheer;
But our hearts would lose their tenderness,
If we never shed a tear.

Our father tests us often,
With suffering and sorrow;
He tests us not to punish us,
But to help us meet tomorrow.

For growing trees are strengthened,
When they withstand the storm;
And the sharp cut of a chisel,
Gives the marble grace and form.

God never hurts us needlessly,
And he never wastes our pain;
For every loss he sends us,
Is followed by rich gain.

And when we count the blessings,
That God has so freely sent;
We will find no cause for murmuring,
And no time to lament.

For our father loves his children,
And to him all things are plain;
So he never sends us pleasure,
When the soul's deep need is pain.

So whenever we are troubled
And when everything goes wrong;
It is just God working in us,
To make our spirit strong.

God's ultimate power is truly formidable, incredible, amazing and life-changing. When I read the words of this powerful poem, I am immediately reminded of another great poet and writer, Lord Byron. One of the most powerful passages written by Lord Byron states the following: "From my youth upward, my spirit walked not with the souls of other men nor looked upon the earth with human eyes. The aim of their existence was not mine; the thirst of their ambition was not mine. My joys, my griefs, my passions and my powers made me a stranger."

Given our current state of affairs, we see people clamoring to win at all costs. That is the way of the world. It is not the way of Christ. Many of our leaders have no moral conscience and they have no principles on which to stand. To them, words like integrity and truth have no significant value. If they don't like the truth, they won't acknowledge it. They merely say what their followers want to hear for they know that not to do so is perilous for them. These people have no vision, no backbone and their egos are far too fragile. Their lack of vision leads them straight into the pit of hell.

True leaders are ones who look beyond the limiting moments of popularity. The great writer, Ralph Waldo Emerson, said it best with these words. "How quickly we succumb to badges and names, large societies and dead institutions." "What I must do is all that concerns me. Not what people think. This rule equally arduous in actual and in intellectual life may serve for the whole distinction between greatness and meanness. It is the harder because you will always find those who think they know your duty better than you know it. It is easy in the world to live after the world's opinions and it is easy in solitude to live after our own; but the great man is he who in the midst of the crowd keeps with perfect sweetness the independence of solitude."

Faith

The master key to riches,
Revealed by the sages;
Can be activated fully,
Through the wisdom of the ages.

Faith is the prerequisite,
Designed to conquer all;
Through universal principles,
Beckoning your call.

Faith is the gift of knowing,
It shatters spiteful doubt;
With bold, intrepid action,
Unmatched in scope and clout.

Faith is demonstrated,
When you show that you believe;
The more it's activated,
The more you will achieve.

When you cultivate your faith,
Believing that you can;
You are building a foundation,
To support your awesome plan.

Release seed faith abundantly,
And watch your ideas grow;
Cultivate them openly,
And share the gift of flow.

Faith is activated,
When you ask for what you seek;
You cannot please the master,
If your show of faith is weak.

The Case for Christ

In the New Testament, Christ provides his followers with an open invitation to follow his lead. It is his gentle promptings and scriptural reminders and still, small voice that demonstrates his unconditional love for us. The greatest, most magnanimous purpose of all is love. John 14:6 says it this way. "I am the way, the truth and the life. No one comes to the father except through me. Let me build the case for Christ. His deity is sovereign.

What separates Jesus Christ from every other being on the planet lies in the fact that he took on the sins of the world, was hung on the cross, died, was buried and on the 3rd day was resurrected. He did all of that to reconcile us back to God when man fell from grace through his sinful nature. No other being or entity on the planet has done that. No one has the power that Christ does.

The uniqueness of Christ resides in the fact that he is both spirit and human. No other being can claim that. This is pointed out specifically in John 1:14. "And the word was made flesh and dwelt among us, {and we beheld his glory, the glory as the only begotten of the father,} full of grace and truth."

Although God is sovereign, which means that he has absolute power and control over everything, still, he does not force you to follow his lead or examples. He gives you the power of free will to make the choices you desire under your own volition. Yet, he stands ready to give you the gift of eternal life once you've made the decision to accept him as Lord and Savior of your life. We are all required to work out our own salvation. The personal relationship that you establish with Jesus Christ is between you and him alone.

Your public acknowledgement of it is a symbol of the love you show to demonstrate your obedience to his will for your life. When you get baptized, you are simply acknowledging to the world that you have made the decision to follow the teachings of

Jesus Christ. When you take the opportunity to walk with the Holy Spirit who finds it impossible to fail, you win.

Allowing God's word to saturate your mind and infiltrate your heart affects the way you act. The more you hide God's word in your heart from the scriptural passages you read, the songs you hear or listen to the powerful wisdom from the sermons you accept into your spirit, the stronger you become as a Christian.

You essentially experience the invisible peace that is not comprehensible to those who have no connection to the Holy Spirit. You can't see the electrical current from God's word that flows through your being but you can feel it and you can reap the tremendous benefits of its powerful manifestation and connectivity through faith. The existing current is right there. His power-driven words, grace and mercy can flow miraculously through your veins.

The more you develop a personal relationship with God, the more your mind can embrace and build a solid, conceptual framework that is designed to lead and guide you on your spiritual journey throughout the entirety of your life. God is not going to force you to walk in his purpose, his will and the path that he has designed for your life; instead, you will come into the knowledge of that gradually. The choices you make along life's journey become the ultimate determining factors in the outcomes and results you experience.

What's truly amazing about the process that God has in place lies in the fact that when you take the time to proactively communicate with God, right at the time you need it most, God will bring to your mind's remembrance those words that were designed to give you the most comfort or to bring the most clarity to your decision-making process. Through diligent study, prayer, asking, seeking and knocking for guidance, you will further refine that process.

The more your faith increases in what God has planned and purposed for you, the more effective you will become as you walk in that purpose. God's blessings and his abundance are unlimited.

Many times, your reward will be in direct proportion to your level of belief.

Although God is incredibly serious-minded about righteousness, he possesses a light-hearted sense of humor as he gives you insights into his persona. I think he does this on purpose just to see if we're paying attention or dismiss his points as something flippant.

Let me give you a couple of examples of what I mean. Here they are. Have you ever thought about the fact that God is always a part of something that's good? Have you ever tried to spell the word "good" without spelling "God"? Hmmm.
What about the word "rich?" Have you ever noticed that the word "rich" is hidden in the word "Christ"? Hmmm. That's really something to think about, isn't it? Perhaps I'm overstating the obvious. Still, it's something to think about for a moment, isn't it?

As I close this final chapter in making the case for Christ, I don't think it's just a coincidence that the word "Christ" contains six letters, or the same number of days it took God to create the world. I think that was by design. Remember, he rested on the seventh.

I paced the floor wondering how to end this chapter and waiting on God's guidance. I thought maybe I would use an acronym for Christ. At first, I thought, Nah! That's too trite or cliché. But then, God took over. That's when I knew it wasn't me but him working through me. Goodness! What an amazing feeling I get that runs from head to foot every time that happens. With that said, I share with you what the Holy Spirit has placed on my heart as an acronym for Christ, a symbol of love and enlightenment for God's creation.

CARE

"For I know the plans I have for you, "declares the Lord" Plans to prosper you and not to harm you. Plans to give you hope and a future. Jeremiah 29:11.

HOPE

"Hope is commonly used to mean a wish: Its strength is the strength of the person's desire. But in the Bible, hope is the confident expectation of what God has promised and its strength is in his faithfulness. The evidence resides in Isaiah 40:31. "They that wait upon the Lord shall renew their strength. They shall mount up with wings as eagles. They shall walk and not be weary. They shall run and not faint."

RESILIENCE

"Blessed is the man that endureth temptation: for when he is tried, he shall receive the crown of life, which God hath promised to them that love him." James 1:2

INSPIRATION

"All scripture is given by inspiration of God, and is profitable for doctrine, for reproof, for correction, for instruction in righteousness: 2 Timothy 3:16.

"That the man of God may be perfect, thoroughly furnished unto all good works." 3:17.

The Bible in its entirety, the unadulterated word of God is your specific road map to success in the physical world as we know it and spiritually as God reveals it to our minds, hearts and souls.

SALVATION

Salvation {From Latin: Salvatio, from Salva, safe, saved.} is the state of being saved or protected from harm or a dire situation. In religion and theology, salvation generally refers to the deliverance of the soul from sin and its consequences. The academic study of salvation is called soteriology.

KJV Romans 10:9-10

"That if thou shalt confess with thy mouth the Lord Jesus, and shalt believe in thine heart that God hath raised him from the dead, thou shalt be saved."

"For with the heart man believeth unto righteousness; and with the mouth confession is made unto salvation."

When Paul is in prison, he writes to the Ephesians in the city of Ephesus situated in one of the Turkish regions of the world, he is most clear in his delineation of the power of faith. In no uncertain terms, he conveys God's message with great precision so that man will not unwittingly try to take credit for something that only God himself can manifest or perform. In Ephesians 2:8, it says, "For by grace are ye saved through faith and that not of yourselves: it is a gift of God: And, in Ephesians 2:9, it says, "Not of works, lest any man should boast."

God allowed his son to be the sacrificial lamb whose primary purpose was to reconcile us back to God after we fell from grace through sin. Christ became the door through which we could re-enter as a means of restoring our broken relationship with God. There was nothing we could do to make that happen. That was God's gift to us.

In Ephesians 2:10, Paul further illustrates God's ultimate purpose for man. "For we are his workmanship, created in Christ Jesus unto good works, which God hath before ordained that we should walk in them." In other words, we were to perform his good works even before we were conceived in the womb.

God is so powerful and omniscient that he knew each one of us even before we were formed in the womb. We were predestined to walk in his ways. However, since God gave us freewill, we had to make the choice to allow God to direct the paths of our lives by accepting Jesus Christ as our personal Lord and Savior. It's the restoration process that enables us to fulfill our true destiny.

TENACITY

Do the Godly until your heart catches up. Tenacious means to keep a firm hold of something. To be tenacious in our faith, we must keep a firm hold of our faith every day in all situations. We cannot be distracted. Tenacity requires perseverance and perseverance requires intentionality.

Tenacity is more than endurance; it is endurance combined with the absolute certainty that what we are looking for is going to transpire. Tenacity is more than hanging on, which may be but the weakness of being too afraid to fall off.

To be ultimately successful in any endeavor or undertaking that is tremendously beneficial to yourself and to others in a positive fashion, you must rest with the assurance and knowledge that God Almighty is your ultimate source of power.

Psalms 46:10

"Be still and know that I am God: I will be exalted among the heathen; I will be exalted in the earth."

Philippians 3:13-14
"Brethern, I count not myself to have apprehended: but this one thing I do, forgetting those things which are behind, and reaching forth unto those things which are before, I press to the mark for the prize of the high calling of God in Christ Jesus."

God's Grace

Ever wonder how you made it,
Through the valleys and the hills;
When you stumbled, when you fell,
And you took such awful spills.

There's a reason you're still here,
For your journey's not complete;
Neither pain nor death has claimed you,
Brought you down to pure defeat.

For God's grace has been sufficient,
And his mercy has endured;
When old fear caused you to tremble,
God told your soul to rest assured.

Then came the wind, the rain, the storms,
Fiercely showed their mighty will;
Until the God, our Rock of Ages,
Whispered to them Peace Be Still!

Oh, his grace is still sufficient,
In a world that's lost its way;
All he asks is that you listen,
Then, he'll hear you when you pray.

He's the one who holds the answers,
And your heart with him he'll keep;
Just be wise in your decisions,
For what you sow is what you'll reap.

God Has Purposed You for Great and Amazing Things

God has an awesome vision,
For the things he's purposed you;
You have to listen with intent,
For what he plans to do.

You must pray for understanding,
And the wisdom to decide;
In all thy ways acknowledge him,
And let him be your guide.

Your gifts are so uniquely you,
Designed for you by God;
He's gone ahead to clear the path,
The one that you may trod.

He's given you free will to reign,
To choose another road;
But patience is his virtue,
As he bears the heavy load.

It may take you a lifetime,
To understand your quest;
But tune into your heart's desire,
Then give it all your best.

You'll be an inspiration,
With every breath you breathe;
And master maturation,
Through the legacy you leave.

The more you act on your intentions,
For what the future brings;
The more you'll know he's purposed you,
For great, amazing things.

Closing Thoughts

My hope is that you have been able to find something of significant value in this book that will cause you to seek a closer relationship with God. Perhaps you have found something that speaks to your soul and now for the first time you realize just exactly how real God is and what role he has been playing in your life.

Even if you do not know Jesus Christ, King of Kings and Lord of Lords, I am simply going to ask you to ask Jesus to come into your life at this time. Simply say, "Oh Jesus, I know that I have sinned. I know that I am not perfect but I'm opening up my heart to you and simply asking you to meet me right here at my point of need. Come into my life, work with me, guide me and help me to get to know you so that I may gain eternal life. In Jesus' name, forgive me of my sins and make me whole I pray. Amen."

As my current pastor, Rev. Antonio Neely or First Lady, Minister Veronica Neely would say, "The doors of my father's house are open. You can come by Christian experience, by letter or as a candidate for baptism."

Rev. Neely is the pastor of Pleasant Green Baptist Church located in Portsmouth, Ohio at 1421 Waller Street. There are other churches in Portsmouth, Ohio and in other states and cities. If you live in another part of the country, I encourage you to unite with another church home so that you may be able to grow abundantly and spiritually. Begin building a powerful relationship with God.

If you are sick or ill, pray and ask him to heal your body. Cultivate that relationship and watch him work a miracle in your life and in the life of someone else for which you truly love and care. It would be the greatest gift you could give to them. Pick up your Bible and just read the comforting word of God for yourself and see what a difference it can make in the quality of your life. God is waiting for you to build a relationship with him. We live in a new time period. God is everywhere. You can find him on

Facebook, Linkedin, Google, Youtube or better yet, when you pray. Keep an open mind and heart and just let Jesus come into your life.

"Study to show thyself approved to God, a workman that needeth not be ashamed, rightly dividing the word of truth." 2nd Timothy 2:15.

About the Author

Dr. Robert L. Lawson has amassed over fifty years of experience serving as a teacher, administrator, adjunct professor, business entrepreneur, consultant, and writer. He began his educational career as an instructor at Gallia Academy High School and taught there in the field of English before moving on to Marshall University and serving as the director of continuing education for thirteen years. Shawnee State University came calling, and he served as the director of continuing education there for seven years before opening his own consulting firm to conduct empowerment training for eight years. He returned to the classroom at Georgetown Jr-Sr. High school and spent nine years there before taking a position at Chillicothe High School at the request of then Principal Dr. Jeffrey Fisher and Superintendent Jon Saxton. After that, he taught an additional two years at the Ohio Valley Christian School in Gallipolis, Ohio under the leadership of Principal Patrick O'Donnell. Dr. Lawson is also a frequent presenter in church settings and spends Sundays and other days sharing ideas on faith, leadership and God's purpose for your life. He is an exceptionally gifted conference presenter for pastors, church auxiliary leaders and so much more.

Dr. Lawson holds a bachelor's degree with a major in English and a minor in speech from the University of Rio Grande, a master's degree from Marshall University with a concentration in 17th century literature, and a doctoral degree from Nova Southeastern University in the field of educational administration.

He has developed and taught numerous curriculums in the field of human potential, growth, and development, which includes such topics as how to stay motivated to win, maximizing your potential for greatness, change your thinking, changing your life, how to make an effective presentation, becoming an effective leader, achieving excellence in the classroom, nuggets of wisdom and daring to be a millionaire. In addition, he has co-authored *Oh Yes We Can! Black Achievement in America* with Gene Murphy, a publication that contains sixteen hundred questions and answers on the African-American experience. Dr. Lawson's most recent publication is entitled *Activate Your Faith: God Has Purposed You for Great and Amazing Things.*

Additional books authored by Dr. Lawson include *The Power of Optimism, The Triumph of the Spirit, Ageless Wisdom, The Gamer, Dare to be a Millionaire, The Dare to be a Millionaire Quotebook, What Every Teenager Needs to know about money, Piggy Back Basics for Kids, Destined for Greatness, Greatness Awaits: Putting Your Dreams into Action and Achieving Excellence in the Classroom.*

Dr. Lawson is considered a scholar with an abundance of expertise in the field of human potential development. He is an outstanding presenter and professional speaker who mixes humor with wit, inspiration and fact while leaving audiences both spellbound and empowered. He currently lives in Portsmouth, Ohio with his lovely wife, Debbie. He is also the proud father of three amazing sons, Robert, James and Michael.

When he is not teaching or lecturing, he is giving empowerment presentations around the globe. His most requested keynote address is *"Destined for Greatness."* His email address is rlawson68@hotmail.com and his current mailing address is PO Box 2052, Portsmouth, Ohio 45662. You can also text him at 740-456-7416

Printed in the USA
CPSIA information can be obtained
at www.ICGtesting.com
LVHW021625061023
760215LV00002B/59